COMIC THERAPY: A PSYCHOTHERAPEUTIC TREATMENT

DORATHY MARINA AND KISHORE

ISBN 979-888629070-7

"To change the world, I need a graphic pen. And to change my mood, I use graphic books."

- DORATHY MARINA

"My friend Dora often tells me more than others,"If I wanna heal myself, my best companion is comics."

-KISHORE

Contents

Foreword

My students Dorathy Marina and Kishore did good research with dedication and created this masterpiece. They have previously achieved success in volunteering programmes, but this is their first experience in the research realm. People undergoing mental stress will be able to explore new perspectives and opportunities with the book titled "Comic Therapy: A Psychotherapeutic Treatment." Eventually, they will realize they can heal themselves.

Throughout my teaching and counselling career, I have noticed that the world has become increasingly busy, and people do not seem to have the courage to confront their mental illnesses. Hopefully, this piece of writing will leave an impression on readers' minds, and they will use it in their daily lives.

\- **Dr P. Christina Ruby Stella,**
Assistant professor, Holy Cross College.

Preface

According to John Ridley,"There are still some people out there who believe comic books are nothing more than, well, comic books. But the true cognoscenti know graphic novels are - at their best - an amazing blend of art literature and the theater of the mind." Art has evolved therapeutically in the past decade. The form of expressive therapy uses the creative process of making art to improve a person's physical, mental, and emotional well-being. Professional art therapists can support individual, family, and community treatments. Cognitive and sensorimotor functions can be improved through art therapy, while self-esteem, self-awareness, emotional resilience, insight, social skills, conflict resolution, and societal change are advancing through art therapy. Secondly, A form of art therapy that uses a comic book format provides an opportunity for a person facing mental illness is Comic therapy. Graphic medicine is a medium that combines comics and discourse about medicine. Today Graphic medicine is popular among most countries. The practitioners are working on a collection of comics serving not only as therapeutic tools for patients but also as educational materials for students. Over the years, graphic medicine has become increasingly relevant. As a result, the use of comic book therapy its functions has also grown. Several clinical and educational settings use comic books and graphic novels alike today, perhaps their ability to meet a variety of needs for a wide range of target audiences. This book covers the sprout to the bloom of Comic Therapy.

    -Author

Acknowledgements

First, I would like to thank everyone who helped me write a book. I'd also like to thank many people who have helped me learn and practise art and design. My special thanks to Kishore, my co-author, who helped me throughout the process. I could not have done this without your help and passion for Comics. An additional thanks to the Notionpress publishing team for gifting the opportunity to convey the unpopular therapy of art.

Prologue

COMIC THERAPY: The combination of art and therapy

THIS BOOK FIRST arises in the Idea on a Volunteering programme SHEPHERD in Yagapudaiyanpatti A village in Tamilnadu, when its authors notice the people of that village using comics as their recreation. We are best friends from our college days, who have discussed making an under search about "the role comics in mental relief" for the first time apart from studies. As a team, we accomplished this book with the help of each other. In examining the start-up for comic therapy, Early art therapy was identified as the pedestal. We ask ourselves things like: What is Comic Therapy and how it can be used among different mentalities? Is Comic therapy in the practical world? How to use comics as a Therapy? At some point in our conversation, the intriguing word "Graphic Medicine" popped up. This concept denotes the role that comics can play in healthcare and, over time, it has been adopted as the accepted term for this area of study and practice. Interestingly, this activity gave us an explanation of art therapy from ancient times to the present. Our research led us to discover that there are many graphic medicines available with different concepts from the fields of psychology combined with comics. Using comics in medicine enables patients to explore their perceptions of health, better understand treatment options, and destigmatize illnesses. The comic medium, which combines words with images, makes it accessible and empathic to tell these personal stories, and even to contain clinical information. Finally, we decided to study the concept from the scratch. We began writing the book after a year of reviewing. A triadic interaction of the art therapist, the client, and the artwork can be deemed to be the constituents of art therapy interventions and add a third dimension to the therapeutic alliance between them. There is some conflicting research regarding the effectiveness of art therapy, but some research suggests it may be beneficial. Research on how and when art therapy may be most valuable is usually small and inconclusive, which requires further study.The purpose of this book is to showcase the comic used in therapy. Such comics are effective at helping those who discover the problem regain self-confidence. So this book delivers the importance of such a comic. It is a composition of every aspect of Comic Therapy. Healing yourself is interconnected with healing others. Aside from making us happy, laughter has numerous health benefits as well. A good laugh is a state of complete body engagement and mind release. The act of connecting to other people heals us by itself. Let's share our laughter through comics. "Smile, it's free therapy!"

- DORATHY MARINA AND KISHORE

CHAPTER ONE

Emergence: Origin and Characteristics of Comic Therapy

Comic book therapy is an art therapy approach were those undergoing rehabilitation or who have successfully completed rehabilitation tell personal stories using comics. Patients can process memories and emotions through the fusion of text and image, two different yet complementary mediums. Psychotherapeutic use of comic book therapy involves having clients read specific comic books, usually surrounding topics similar to their own diagnoses. It is encouraged for clients to present their thoughts and feelings while reading along with how those experiences relate to their own lives. One attempts to reach a cathartic moment during which one realizes their own life. It is possible to use therapeutic methods of both types throughout the patient's treatment process: from the moment of diagnosis to rehabilitation, and during the events that follow, including readjustment and general coping. There are a variety of populations undergoing comic book therapy, including patients diagnosed with life-altering conditions. The US Defense Advanced Research

Projects Agency is currently developing a therapy concept originally proposed by Captain Russel Shilling.

EnRussel Shilling illustrated by Dorathy Marina

Following the First World War and just after the completion of the comics industry was established in the early 1920s. The subsequent years witnessed an explosion of comics editions that remain popular today with children and adults alike familiarizing themselves with Superheroes like Superman, Batman and Spiderman. Comic books and comic book characters.became even more popular with the development of radio and television. The merchandising of comic books saw an all-time high. With the advent of comic books, select topics of academia have slowly begun to matriculate into comic books, now considered important forms of literary expression covering topics including medicine, politics, economy, and social change.

Spiderman and Superman illustrated by DORATHY MARINA

The story of comics can be traced back to the early 1920s, however, by professionals within the graphic medicine field. However, they claim that their field, origins lie in prehistoric cave drawings and the desire of mankind to express themselves with pictures. The historians of comic books tend to see Egyptian hieroglyphics, Mayan drawings, Aztec drawings, and the great art of the Greeks, the Persians, and the Romans as part of the history of comic books.

MAYAN DRAWINGS and EGYPTIAN HIEROGLYPHICS Designed by freepik

Multicultural forms of expression and communication, art holds several therapeutic properties. Since archaeologists have discovered more evidence and new sites found in caves from the Paleolithic period, it is clear that Neanderthals carved markings of varying shapes and sizes onto cave walls- the earliest forms of art (Than, 2012). Packard (1980) thinks humans from this period used art as a psychological prepping tool for preparing for their long and dangerous hunting expeditions. Symbolic offerings to their gods, these paintings depict the hunter's fears, hopes, and wishes. In addition, it has been suggested that art in the Paleolithic period served a variety of purposes, including narratives, myths, messages, and games (Bahn, 1996). Over time, what began as a way for people to express their creative needs became something we consider sometimes necessary when words fail to adequately communicate our feelings and inner emotions. People who lived in prehistoric civilizations also valued art as a means of personal development and survival.. It was common practice in ancient Egypt to create art for religious purposes and to symbolically depict the afterlife. Hieroglyphs were also used to communicate in ancient Egypt. Likewise, Greeks used hieroglyphs to communicate. The art they created represented both their religious beliefs and everyday life.

PALEOLITHIC PERIOD designed by freepik

Hybridizing art and psychology, art therapy encourages people in therapy to develop self-awareness, explore emotions, resolve unresolved emotional conflicts, improve their social skills, and boost their self-esteem as a result of the creative process and artwork created in therapy. The purpose of art therapy is primarily to help individuals experiencing emotional and psychological problems develop personal well-being and function more effectively. There is no requirement for prior artistic experience or innate artistic ability for art therapy to be successful. Art therapy can be helpful to anyone seeking treatment from a mental health professional. Through history, art has served as a form of communication, self-expression, group interaction, diagnosis, and conflict resolution. People from cultures and religions around the world have incorporated carved idols and charms into the healing process for centuries, along with sacred paintings and symbols. It took several decades for art therapy to become a publically accepted therapeutic approach. Throughout Europe and the United States, art therapy emerged independently and simultaneously as a profession. Adrian Hill, a British artist who recovered from tuberculosis in 1942, coined the term "art therapy." Several mental health practitioners in the 1940s began to describe their work with patients as "art therapy." Since there were no formal art therapy courses or training programs available at the time, caring providers were often trained in other disciplines and supervised by psychiatrists, psychologists, or other mental health professionals.

Art Versus Illness: A Study of Art Therapy Adrian Hill

In art therapy, comics are used as therapeutic tools. One way to provide comic book therapy is to encourage patients, their support systems, and their healthcare providers to read already published graphic novels and comic books. In parallel with the growth of graphic medicine, comic books and novels have also grown in popularity. Therefore, the topics covered in graphic novels and comic books today range from cancer, to Parkinson's disease, to schizophrenia, Alzheimer's disease, to eating disorders, etc. Cancer Vixen: a True Story by Marisa Acocella Marchetto, Tangles: A Story About Alzheimer's, My Mother, and Me by Sarah Leavitt, and Marbles: Mania, Depression, Michelangelo, and Me by Ellen Forney are popular novels. Novels that share similar experiences, diagnoses, and personal histories with those of their patients are recommended by therapists. The intention is for the patients to try to draw parallels between their own experiences and those in the panels. Unlike simply reading a recommended autobiography, this approach goes beyond simple reading. Each panel contains images and graphics that help complete the narrative by bridging the gap between words and meaning. The way in which an author depicts their characters, their plot, and their environment all contribute greatly to the reading experience.

Cancer Vixen: a True Story by Marisa Acocella Marchetto

After this brief overview of the introduction to topics covered in this book, Several ancient arts are examined, along with the history of Art Therapy, and considerations regarding Comic Therapy are taken into account.

CHAPTER TWO

Aims and Sequel: Why Graphic Medicine?

These personal stories, including clinical information, are made more approachable and emotionally impactful by the own language of phrases and images that are part of the comic outlet. In graphic medicine, a personal experience of illness and fitness is conveyed, with the art adding subjective, emotional significance to the story. Internal, personal opinions of the author balance the external, clinical realm of medical symptoms and diagnoses. Furthermore, it's a way so that other patients who have the same health issue can stay in touch and exchange information.

Dr. Ian Williams describes Graphic Medicine as "the intersection of the medium of comics and the discourse of healthcare."

A comic's language combines the explicit meaning of words and symbols with the conceptual expressiveness of art. On the other hand, looking at the comics, the text and images work together to create meaning that neither signifies alone. Aside from visual analogy and combined or altered symbols, comics use humor as well as other storytelling elements. A story can be enriched with infographics of particular clinical information by weaving in the author's own experiences. An author's ability to understand illness and treatment can help him or her cope and recover, and conveying that knowledge to readers can help change a negative experience into a positive experience. An inherent part of being a victim is handling the nature care system, which is characterized in some examples of graphic therapy. For health authorities, families, and the public, the insight given by these articles can offer useful feedback to health care providers and promotes beneficial treatment. As well as racism and discrimination, comic books deal with war, envy, friendship, and an individual's sense of responsibility. It is especially important in today's political climate to portray superheroes as representations of ourselves. These characters are complex, emotional, and possess a vast array of skills. Comic books are stories, and stories are incredibly powerful and influential. Comic books can be used in counseling in many related settings, from personal therapy to group therapy. Comic books can be used as bibliotherapy. As we become a part of them, they become a part of us. Reading and reflecting on specific issues can be the basis for bibliotherapy. Following the client's reading and reflection, the stories can be filtered in the counseling session. The stories in comic books may also indicate how to apply moral strength and resilience in making a positive change. It is possible to open up in ways that they didn't think were possible when reading comics.

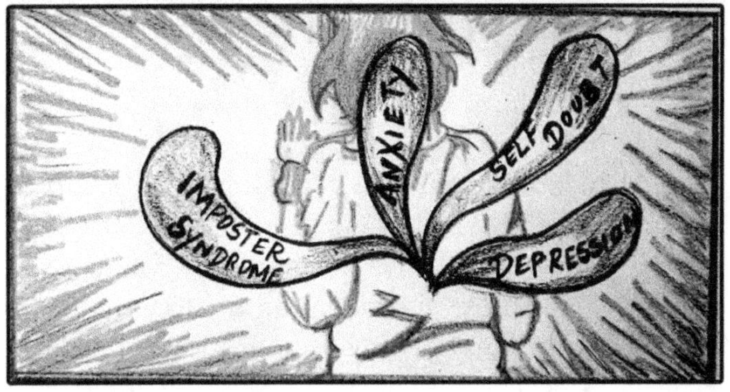

Illustrated by DORATHY MARINA

According to a 2016 study published in the Journal of the American Art Therapy Association,less than an hour of creative activity can reduce your stress and have a positive effect on your mental health, regardless of artistic experience or talent.

CHAPTER THREE

Modus Operandi : Interaction of graphic storytelling in the clinical field

Comprehending, education, information, investigation, meaning-making, examination, sympathy, diversity/ cultural ability, community, ethics, and therapy are just a few reasons why graphic medicine has important applications. In terms of expanding and developing, graphic medicine is beneficial from two perspectives. In graphic medicine, meaning is created by interpreting an experience to give it meaning, understanding, and/or finding 'Truth' among the experiences. This is following the innovation of graphic medicine in this case. It allows students and healthcare professionals to analyze past experiences by creating comics. Their coping mechanisms often help them deal with the pressures of healthcare. Families and patients are also affected by this. An illustration of a medical incident can provide closure or perspective. Several explanations can be given for all of these. Communication, education, and research are all connected through understanding. It may mean informing a sympathetic and/or family member about current data about a modern or occurring illness. Essentially, teaching health to students of all ages is one way of accomplishing this.

Illustrated by DORATHY MARINA

n addition to communicating health information, graphic medicine can also be used to enhance the lives of people with health conditions and their families. Using graphic medicine offers an alternative approach to addressing health conditions. A comic can help increase an individual's understanding of health conditions.The mixture of illustrations and written information helps the reader understand and memorize the topics. It also provides a better connection to the characters. This helps with empathy and population. It provides the impression that you are not the only one out there grasping this. Graphic medicine can improve communication and empathy between healthcare specialists and patients. Health professionals examining graphic medicine, particularly titles about the patient or family experience, are better able to sympathize with and connect to patients and their families.

This comic strip drawn by Jessica Abel in 2002 is a great introduction to what comics are, how they work, and how to read them.

The storytelling genre encompasses both fiction and nonfiction. The ubiquity of comics in popular culture is at an all-time high; it is not only adapted to movies, but also to television and stage productions. It is also used as a teaching tool across all academic disciplines. There is a growing section of comics publishing dedicated to autobiographical and medical narratives, which is of interest to the medical professions. Williams coined the term "graphic medicine" in 2007 for comics that tell the stories of illness and health through medical narratives embedded in the narratives of patients and caregivers. In this sense, graph medicine is a form of narrative medicine. It is a method of teaching and learning that has been recognized as a way to encourage healing in medical practice. A comic book is a form of literature that uses the language of images and words in combination to convey meaning that only they can convey. There has been a growing interest in graphic medicine narratives among medical doctors, leading to the development of a graphic medicine conference and publications of these narratives in major medical journals. Health professions education has undergone a fundamental transformation in recent years, redefining both the learning process and the way in which self-expression can be expressed for both educators and learners. This commentary familiarize pharmacy educators with the concept of graphic medicine and to point out areas in which graphic medicine is useful as a teaching tool in the pharmacy curriculum. Graphic novels have grown in popularity in recent years, and a number of titles deal directly with patients' experiences of illness or caring for others who suffer from illness. Medical schools now encourage students to read classic literature as a way of gaining insight into the human condition in part due to the Medical Humanities movement. In spite of the fact that some authors argue that graphic fiction is a form of literature, the medium of comics (both physical objects and the philosophy and practice surrounding them) has received little attention from healthcare scholars. Researchers propose it is time to examine some acclaimed comic works and have healthcare professionals examine the medium. With reference to narrative medicine, this aims to determine whether comics and graphic novels can be useful as a resource for health professionals, patients, and caregivers.

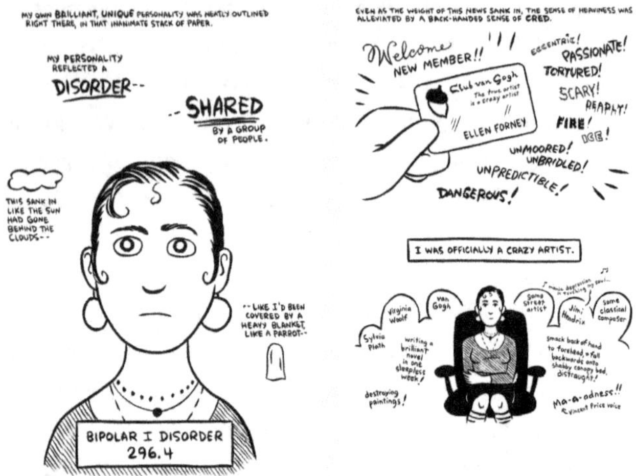

From Marbles: Mania, Depression, Michelangelo, and Me, Ellen Forney, 2012 Courtesy Ellen Forney

CHAPTER FOUR

Offshoot: Kind of Comic Therapy and its Benefits

Originally a niche phenomenon, this is now a widespread manifestation that connects people from all walks of life. The purpose of comics doesn't have to be purely entertaining. The use of graphic novels for therapy aids can be beneficial to those who have physical and mental disorders. As a therapeutic tool, comic books have a range of benefits, which is why The Comic Vault is exploring ways for them to be used. Graphic tales are a powerful form of escapism and have many medicinal benefits. In addition to providing comfort to patients, the story may reduce their stress levels. Developing a comic or graphic novel can be one aspect of comic therapy. This involves investigating the various methods of art and text with a therapist, family member, or support group. By looking beyond text-based storytelling, a victim establishes something that helps in the treatment process. Therapy with comics encourages readers to be imaginative and accepted by themselves. Having a patient relate with a single personality is a big step forward, and that, in my opinion, is the essence of therapy.

To reach a breakthrough, patients and their therapists can work together one step at a time. Comics also encourage creativity, and patients may agree they want to analyze different forms of writing. An example would be a journal where a patient logs their emotions to understand what they are going through.

Partients can design their own comics or graphic novels as part of comic therapy. In this process, a therapist, family member of support group explores themedium of art and text. Creating somethings that helps the healing process extends beyond text-based storytelling. Mentally ill people can be encourged to create a comic based on their own experiences. As a result, they will be able to rewrite theirown story and do things differently. A patient may be able to experience an emotional breakthroughthrough comics, becausethe medium provides a safe environment where there are no consequences to the patient's actions. It is best to start off by developing the characters and thinking about how you can use your experiences to help them. Reading and connecting with characters in a graphic novel is a traditional kind of comic therapy. In addition to being great role models. superheroes serve as a reflection of society. A superhero like Captain America gives you hope. Patients can also perceive their issues in a character's behavior, whether it is physical or mental.

MY NAME IS DR. HENRY PYM. I DISCOVERED HOW TO SHRINK AND ENLARGE MATTER AND, SO, NATURALLY PUT ON A COSTUME TO FIGHT CRIME.
I WILL EXPLAIN SHORTLY WHY THAT MADE SENSE.

ACTUALLY, SEVERAL COSTUMES, SEVERAL IDENTITIES OVER THE YEARS.
YELLOWJACKET. GOLIATH. GIANT-MAN.
ANT-MAN.

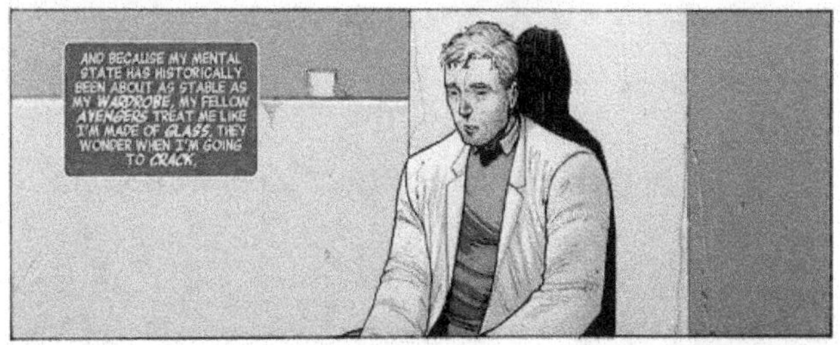
AND BECAUSE MY MENTAL STATE HAS HISTORICALLY BEEN ABOUT AS STABLE AS MY WARDROBE, MY FELLOW AVENGERS TREAT ME LIKE I'M MADE OF GLASS. THEY WONDER WHEN I'M GOING TO CRACK.

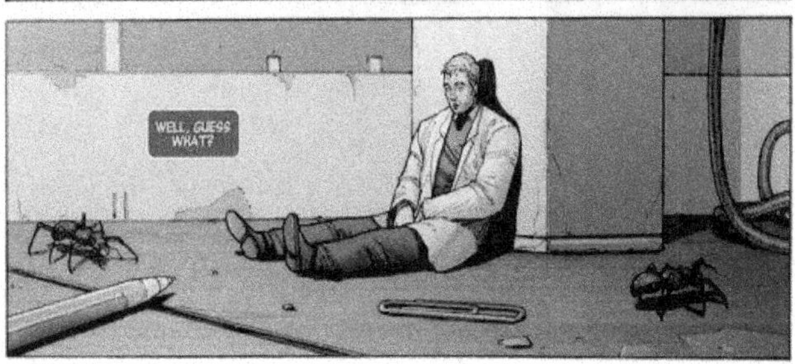
WELL, GUESS WHAT?

An individual suffering from cancer can read The Mighty Thor and relate to Jane Foster, who is battling her disease. In spite of her illness, Jane used her remaining time to make the world a better place by taking on the role of Thor. The reader may be inspired by Jane's journey and find a silver lining within their own lives.

Superhero Therapy is a kind of comic therapy.

There are numerous therapeutic benefits of comic books, with graphic novels serving as an excellent form of escapism. The story can reduce stress and make a patient feel more at ease in their environment. An individual reading a comic can also feel happy and accepted since the struggles they face are viewed in a different light. As the hero overcomes their problems, the reader feels motivated to make their progress. The act of creating comics encourages creativity, and a patient might decide to explore other forms of writing. This might take the form of writing down their emotions in a journal so they can better understand what's going on inside them. As a therapeutic tool, comics can help patients to feel inspired and accepted. If a patient can connect with even one character, that's a small step, and in my opinion, that's the essence of therapy. Comic therapy may often be achieved by those facing issues such as Anxiety, Depression Substance dependency, Stress, Posttraumatic stress, Attention deficit hyperactivity, Cancer, Compassion fatigue Heart disease, Anorexia,Bulimia, Other eating disorders, Cognitive impairments, Family or relationship issues.

From Iggy and The Inhalers, by Alex Thomas, MD, to teach kids with asthma about asthma symptoms, treatment and medication.

CHAPTER FIVE

Superhero Therapy: A Therapy of Recognition and Allegiance

Superhero Therapy is a new form of therapy based on comic book superheroes like Superman and Batman. With their superhuman accomplishments, these heroes have gained a wide following. They are idols to children, who model their lives after them. In adulthood, popularity cannot be lost forever. It has been our experience to grow up longing to be just like them! The characters depict hope and resistance against evil and are born into a world gripped by war in which most countries are involved. Superheroes have been sustaining our subconscious demands for a saviour, which seems to be our subconscious need. Superheroes face harsh realities. However, they remain intact. They win every battle of adversity earning a place of respect in our hearts. Psychiatrists have been trying to leverage this area of "if they can, I can too" grit, inspiring us to help fight mental battles. Hopefully, there is a sunrise somewhere.

Ah, yes, our good friends anxiety, depression, anger and shame. (from 'Superhero Therapy,' art by Wellinton Alves)

In light of the concept's relative infancy, its exact definition has yet to be established. Superhero Therapy can refer to either psychoanalyzing superheroes or employing superheroes in treatment to facilitate recovery in the world of psychology. In varying ways, both can potentially benefit us: the former by helping us understand our favourite characters (for instance, through books like Batman and Psychology: A Dark and Stormy Knight, or The Psychology of Superheroes). Ultimately, this latter by helping us shape our behaviour to recover.

Illustrated by DORATHY MARINA

Superhero Therapy has been used by several therapists, including myself, to treat anxiety disorders, depression, and posttraumatic stress disorder. This is done by incorporating examples from comic books, movies, and TV shows as the means to allow to better understand what he or she is experiencing. Often when someone is struggling with a painful experience it might be difficult to make sense of the present situation. In addition, painful emotional experiences, such as depression or trauma, can potentially be alienating, creating false beliefs that we are the only ones going through this or that no one else will understand. Sometimes recognizing that some of our favourite heroes have been through a similar experience can potentially be healing. Research suggests that when we identify that we have gone through a painful experience just as others have (the concept of common humanity), this can allow us to feel more connected and that connection with others might even inspire physiological changes in the body, such as the release of a hormone, oxytocin, which is related to increased feelings of love and compassion, reduced stress, reduced depression and anxiety, and increased lifespan. Superheros go through challenges and impediments, just like we do. Comic books have evolved more differently, with African American male superheroes such as Sam Wilson (Falcon), Luke Cage, and T'Challa (the Black Panther), as well as Miles Morales (Spider-Man), a male of black and Latino destruction. Comics are also evolving more female-driven. The new "Iron Man" is an old African American female, Riri Williams was a genius. The new Thor, exerting the hammer Mjölnir, is also a woman, Jane Foster. This comic book was contentious because Foster is not called "Lady Thor" or some other female version of the name. Instead, she is Thor, and she is worthy of the mantle.

> TO GIVE CHILDREN AND FAMILIES A MOMENTARY ESCAPE FROM REALITY – WHETHER THEY ARE IN A HOSPITAL ROOM, HOMELESS SHELTER OR MEDICAL TREATMENT
>
> *- Clinical Care Comics, Los Vegas*

The Critical Care Comics, Los Vegas's mission is to Make Kids Smile. The CRITICAL CARE COMICS is a non-profit organization. Their mission is to give children and families a momentary escape from reality – whether they are in a hospital room, homeless shelter or medical treatment facility.

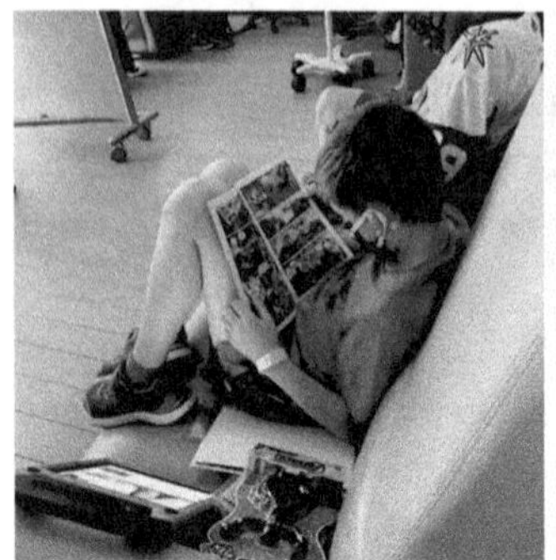 

Conclusion Comic Therapy: The Method Of Artistic Healing

Illustrated by DORATHY MARINA

In Graphic Medicine, comics are used to depict the wide range of experiences of illness, caregiving, and disability. Through comics, we can improve our health by making education more engaging, amplifying the voices of patients and families, and exploring our experiences with health, illness, disability, and caregiving. Graphic Medicine will act as a nurse that can assist patients anywhere and anytime. Comics gives clients the ability to read about themes that they connect to and can help them open up in ways that they didn't think possible. A comic book story can also illustrate moral courage and resiliency as well as a decision to make a positive change. Comic Therapy helps in healing artistically. As individuals are able to display their emotions, it aids in the healing process. Healing and expression in creative aspects can be beneficial to the individuals, as well as the viewer. A person can connect to the piece and find solution to their own trials.

"The experience of reading a printed comic book will never change, but now, thanks to the digital age, there are many different ways to enjoy the same story. Digital comic books, of course, can be interactive in many different ways, allowing the reader to feel like a participant in the story."   - Stan Lee

Suggestions For Further Reading

The authors were greatly inspired by:

It Shouldn't Be This Way: Learning to Accept the Things You Just Can't Change, JANINA SCARLET

Super-Women: Superhero Therapy for Women Battling Anxiety, Depression, and Trauma. JANINA SCARLET

Superhero Therapy Professional GUIDE, JANINA SCARLET

Depresso, Or, How I Learned to Stop Worrying-- and Embrace Being Bonkers, BRICK Comic Nurse, MK CZERWIEC

Menopause: A Comic Treatment, MK CZERWIEC

The Bad Doctor, IAN WILLIAMS

The Lady Doctor, IAN WILLIAMS

Cancer Vixen: A True Story, MARISA ACOCELLA MARCHETTO

Marbles: Mania, Depression, Michelangelo, and Me: A Graphic Memoir, ELLEN FORNEY

Mom's Cancer, BRIAN FIES

About The Authors

DORATHY MARINA is a citizen of India. Bachelor's in Mathematics from St. Joseph's College (Autonomous), Trichy. And have studied different fields like illustration, animation and VFX. She is an author, illustrator and cartoonist.

KISHORE is a citizen of India. Bachelor's in Mathematics from St. Joseph's College (Autonomous), Trichy.